MINDFUL MATH

Use Your ALGEBRA to Solve these Puzzling Pictures

Blackline Masters by Ann McNair

Illustrations by Robyn Djuritschek

Tarquin

PUBLISHER'S NOTE

Tarquin were delighted when Ann and Robyn approached us with the idea for the three books in this series. We have published and sold hundreds of thousands of copies of similar books for younger ages – see below – and had great success with other entertaining approaches to homework, revision and reinforcement. Books such as Mini Mathematical Murder Mysteries, Mathematical Team Games, Mathematical Treasure Hunts and Mathstraks activities – make up a wonderful set of resources for every style of learning and teaching.

The three Mindful Math titles join these books in our Tarquin eReader system, which allows you to add ebooks and then search for what you want so that you can print activities. We heavily discount ebook access for those who buy hard copy books, so they are as easy to use as possible.

See our full range at www.tarquingroup.com, sign up for our newsletters and follow us on Twitter and Facebook @tarquingroup for news, offers and new resources. All our books are available in the USA and Canada through www.ipgbook.com.

OTHER COLORING BOOKS FROM TARQUIN

Mindful Math – Geometry	ISBN 9781913565787
Mindful Math – Statistics	ISBN 9781913565794

For more coloring books for secondary ages, see the **By Design** series on our website

FOR AGES 5-11

Arithmetic Arithmetic	ISBN 9781899618149
The Multiplication Tables Colouring Book	ISBN 9780906212851
The Second Multiplication Tables Colouring Book	ISBN 9781899618309

Published by Tarquin Publications
Suite 74, 17 Holywell Hill
St Albans AL1 1DT, UK

www.tarquingroup.com

Distributed by IPG Books,
814 N. Franklin St.,
Chicago, IL 60610, USA

www.ipgbook.com

Design: Karl Hunt

Printed in the USA

ISBN (Book)   9781913565770
ISBN (EBook) 9781913565800

contents

1
SIMPLIFYING EXPRESSIONS

PART 1: Simplify the expression. Shade in the coefficient of *a*

1. $6a + 3a + 2a$
2. $14a + 2a - 15a$
3. $2 \times 5a$
4. $5a + 3a - a$
5. $7(3a + 4) + 4a - 21$

PART 2: Simplify the expression. Shade in the coefficient of *b*

6. $8(3a + 6b) + b$
7. $10a + 15b - 3a + 26b + 2a$
8. $3(4b - a) + 5(2a + 3b)$
9. $10(2a + 5b) - 2(4a - 10b)$
10. $3b(b + 2)$

PART 3: Simplify the expression. Shade in the constant.

11. $4(2a + 3b + 7)$
12. $5(3a - 2) + 8(a + 8)$
13. $2(7a + 3b - 1) + 3a(a + b + 2) + 6(b + 3) + 1$
14. $2(5a - b) + 6(2a + 2) - 9(a - 9)$
15. $(a + 10)(a + 10)$

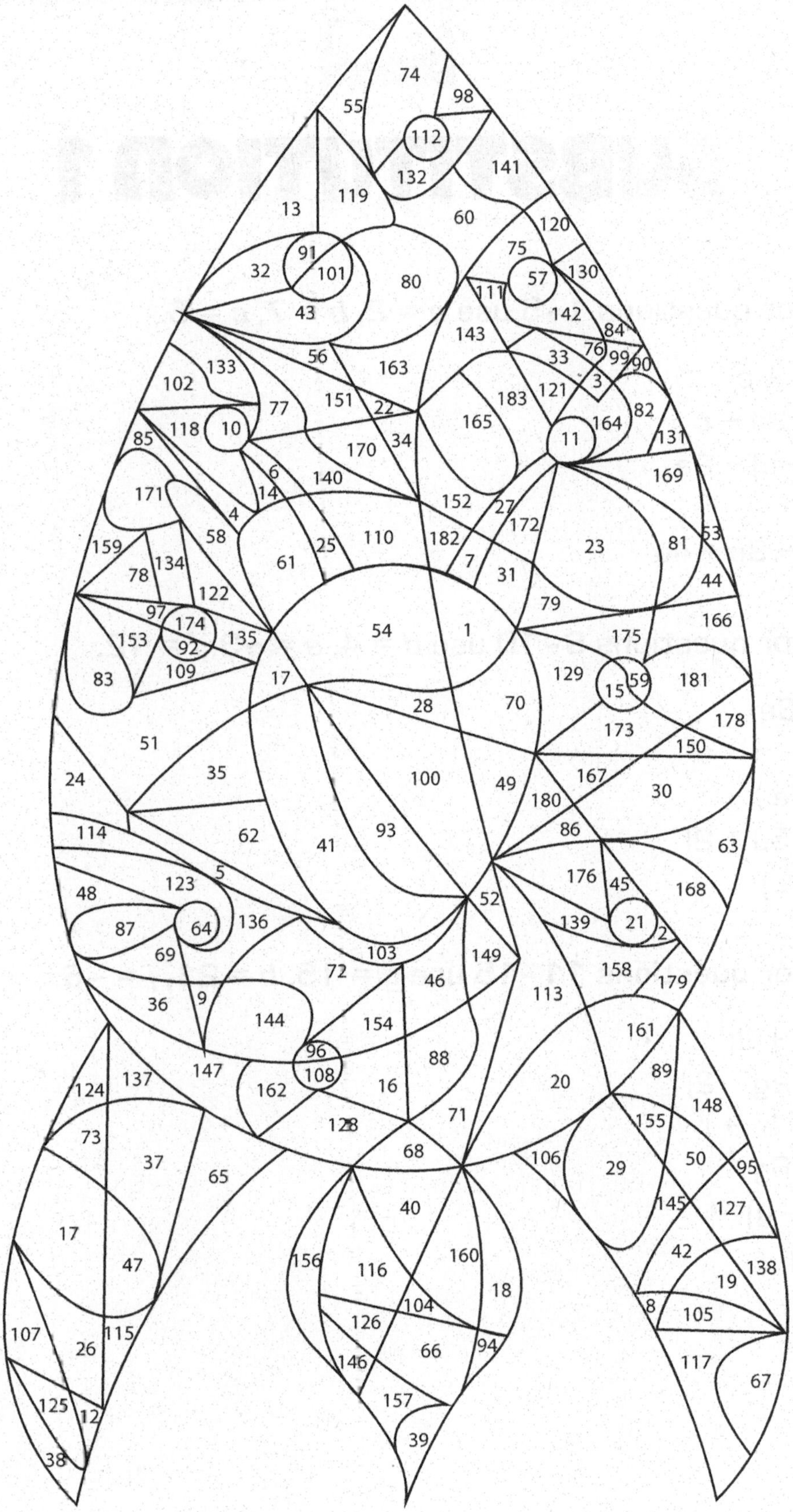
74
98
55
112
141
132
119
13
60
120
75
91
130
32
101
80
57
111
43
142
84
143
56
163
33
76
99
90
133
102
3
121
77
151
22
183
82
118
10
165
164
85
170
34
11
131
6
140
169
171
14
152
27
4
172
53
58
110
182
159
25
81
61
23
134
7
31
78
44
122
79
97
174
166
54
1
135
153
92
175
109
17
129
59
181
83
15
28
70
178
173
51
150
35
167
24
100
49
30
180
114
62
93
41
86
63
5
123
176
45
48
52
168
87
64
136
139
21
2
69
103
149
72
158
46
179
36
9
113
144
154
161
96
147
88
137
124
108
20
89
162
16
148
73
155
128
71
68
37
106
50
65
29
95
40
145
127
17
156
160
116
42
138
47
19
18
104
8
105
107
126
26
115
66
94
146
117
67
157
125
12
39
38

2 SUBSTITUTION 1

PART 1: For questions 1–5 use $a = 2$, $b = 7$, $c = 5$.

1. $a + b + c$
2. $2b + 3a - c$
3. $3(b + c) - 2a$
4. $2c^2$
5. $10b - 3c + 4a$

PART 2: For questions 6–10 use $d = 4$, $e = -3$, $f = 12$.

6. $4f + 3e$
7. $(2e)^2$
8. $d - 2e$
9. $6e + 5d + 2f$
10. $6(f - e)$

PART 3: For questions 11–15 use $g = 15$, $h = 21$, $j = -6$.

11. $g + h + 2j$
12. $3h - 2g - 2j$
13. $2g^2 - h^2 + j$
14. $7h - 6g$
15. $-\dfrac{(h - g)}{j}$

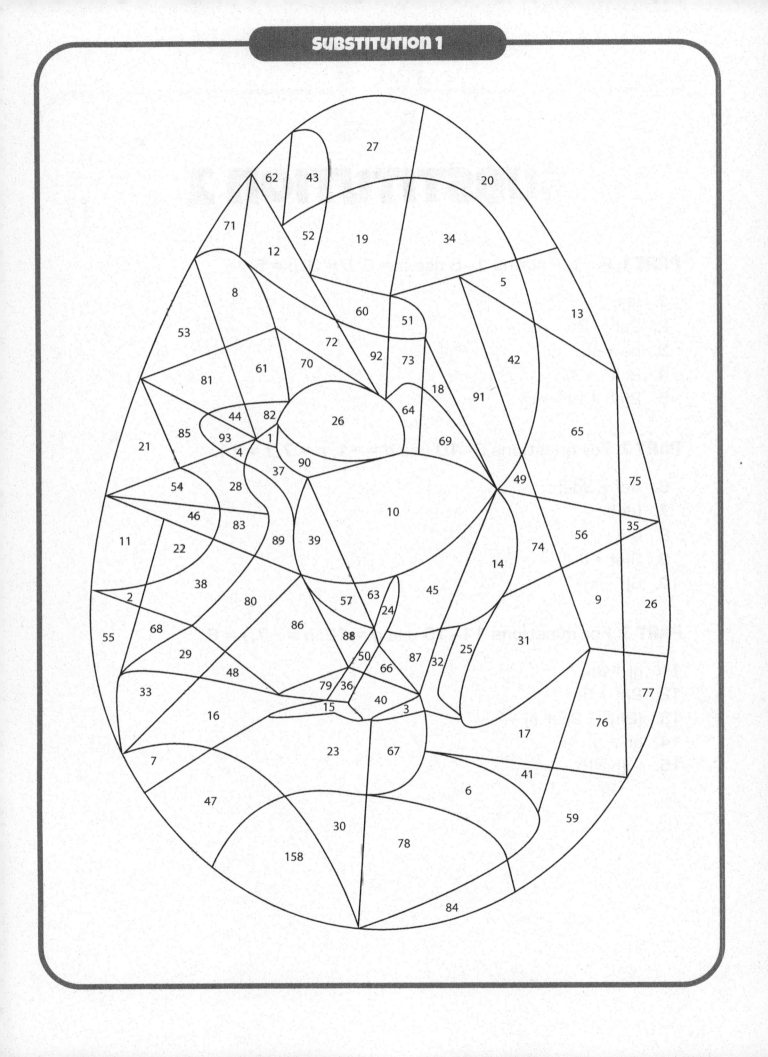

SUBSTITUTION 2

PART 1: For questions 1–5 use $a = 6$, $b = 3$, $c = 5$.

1. abc
2. $2ab - 3c$
3. $bc + ab - ac$
4. $2cb^2 - 3a$
5. $2(ab + 2c) - c^2$

PART 2: For questions 6–10 use $d = -1$, $e = 7$, $f = 11$.

6. $4ef + 3def$
7. $(de)^2$
8. d^2e
9. $3(ef + de^2)$
10. $6(f - e)^2$

PART 3: For questions 11–15 use $g = 12$, $h = -7$, $j = 8$.

11. $gj + 2h$
12. $2g^2 + 5hj$
13. $(2h)^2 - 2j^2 + hj$
14. $gh + gj - h$
15. $-\dfrac{(hg^2)}{2j}$

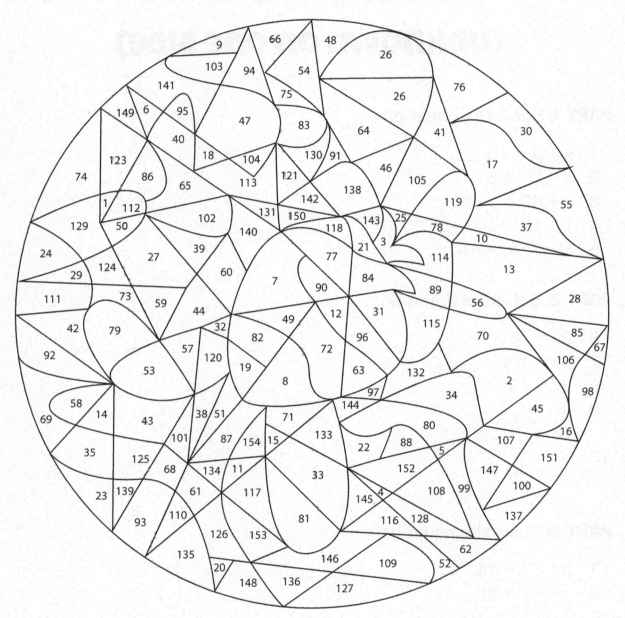

4

SOLVE THE EQUATION 1
(unknown on one side)

PART 1: Solve the equation.

1. $x + 3 = 10$
2. $x - 7 = 25$
3. $x + 42 = 113$
4. $x - 13 = 44$
5. $x - 32 = -20$

PART 2: Solve the equation.

6. $2x = 76$
7. $5x = 100$
8. $8x = 192$
9. $\dfrac{x}{13} = 7$
10. $\dfrac{x}{7} = 10$

PART 3: Solve the equation

11. $2x + 3 = 11$
12. $5x - 7 = 68$
13. $2x + 21 = 109$
14. $\dfrac{2x}{5} + 40 = 66$
15. $\dfrac{3x}{8} - 26 = -11$

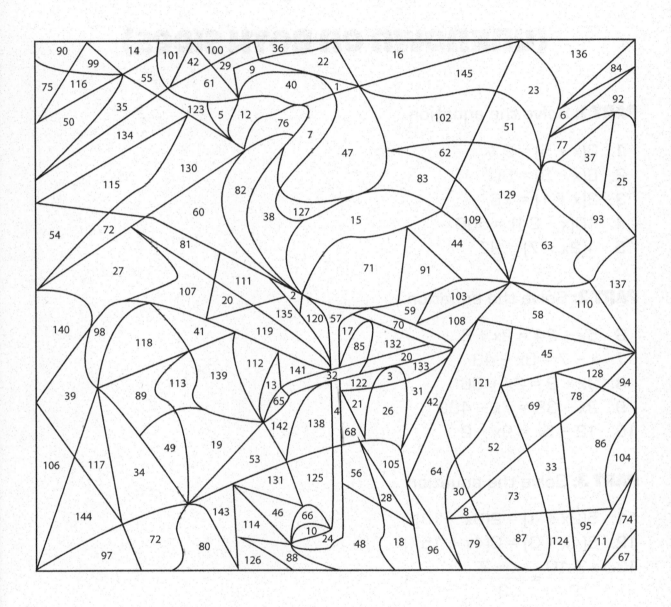

5

SOLVE THE EQUATION 2
(UNKNOWN ON BOTH SIDES)

PART 1: Solve the equation.

1. $3(x + 5) = 27$
2. $6(x - 3) = 60$
3. $2(x + 1) = 76$
4. $10(x - 24) = 500$
5. $4(2x - 7) = 92$

PART 2: Solve the equation.

6. $5x - 24 = 2x + 6$
7. $x - 7 = 3x - 43$
8. $3x + 8 = 2x + 56$
9. $2x - 38 = 7x - 488$
10. $12 - 5x = 9x - 2$

PART 3: Solve the equation

11. $5(2x + 4) = 2(6x - 13)$
12. $5(4x + 3) = 3(4x + 157)$
13. $\dfrac{x + 10}{9} = \dfrac{x - 2}{3}$
14. $\dfrac{x + 2}{x - 15} = \dfrac{4}{3}$
15. $5(6 - x) + 17 = 5 + 7(x - 6)$

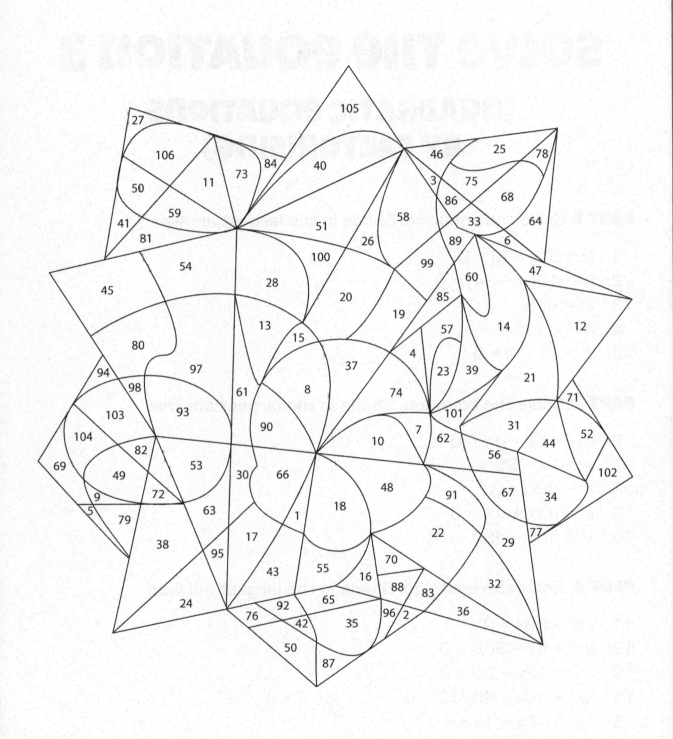

6

SOLVE THE EQUATION 3
(QUADRATIC EQUATIONS BY FACTORISING)

PART 1: Solve the equation. Shade in the largest answer.

1. $(x + 3)(x - 8) = 0$
2. $(x - 10)(x - 34) = 0$
3. $x^2 = 625$
4. $4x^2 = 1296$
5. $x^2 - 2x + 1 = 0$

PART 2: Solve the equation. Shade in the largest answer.

6. $x^2 - 15x + 44 = 0$
7. $x^2 + 2x - 35 = 0$
8. $x^2 - 400 = 0$
9. $x^2 - 42x + 41 = 0$
10. $x^2 + 15x - 480 = 16$

PART 3: Solve the equation. Shade in the largest answer.

11. $2x^2 - 66x = 0$
12. $2x^2 - 6x - 308 = 0$
13. $3x^2 + 12x - 36 = 0$
14. $9x^2 + 18x - 25272 = 0$
15. $12x^2 + 5x - 123 = 0$

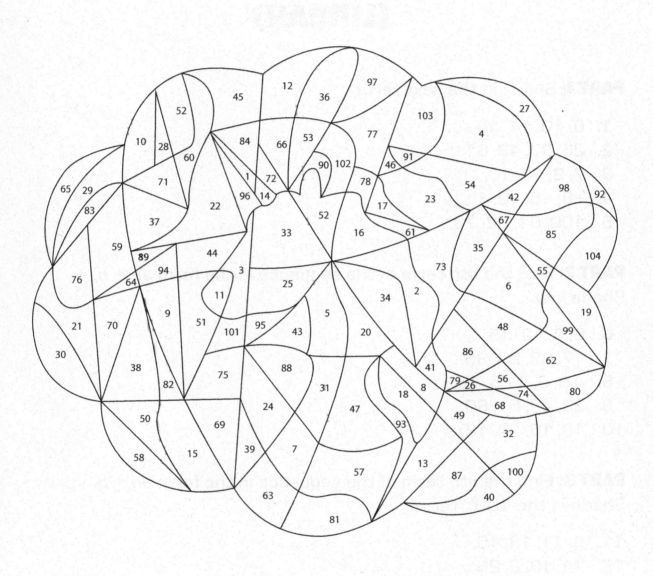

sequences 1
(LineaR)

PART 1: Shade in the next term.

1. 6, 10, 14, 18, . . .
2. 25, 37, 49, 61, . . .
3. 7, 9, 11, 13, . . .
4. −8, −5, −2, 1, . . .
5. 100, 91, 82, 73, . . .

PART 2: Find the *nth* term of the sequence in the form *an* + *b*. Shade in *b*.

6. 6, 9, 12, 15, . . .
7. 17, 23, 29, 35, . . .
8. 4.5, 8, 11.5, 15, . . .
9. 33, 42, 51, 60, . . .
10. 18, 16, 14, 12, . . .

PART 3: Find the *nth* term of the sequence in the form *an* + *b*. Shade in the **100**th term.

11. 9, 11, 13, 15, . . .
12. 14, 18, 2, 26, . . .
13. 4.5, 6, 7.5, 9, . . .
14. 500, 495, 490, 485, . . .
15. 7.5, 8, 8.5, 9, . . .

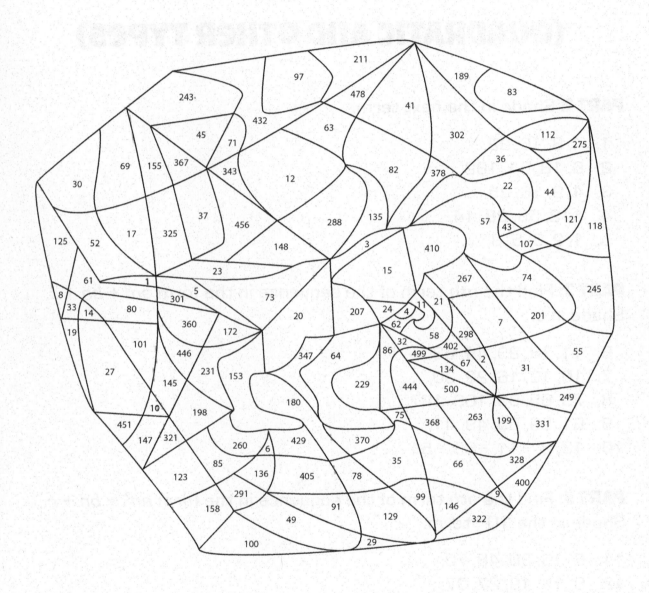

8

sequences 2
(QUADRATIC AND OTHER TYPES)

PART 1: Shade in the next term.

1. 4, 8, 16, 32, . . .
2. 6, 18, 54, 162, . . .
3. 4, 9, 16, 25, . . .
4. 112, 56, 28, 14, . . .
5. 1, 2, 3, 5, 8, . . .

PART 2: Find the *nth* term of the sequence in the form $an^2 + bn + c$. Shade in *c*.

6. 11, 18, 29, 44, 63, . . .
7. 10, 12, 16, 22, 30, . . .
8. 79, 85, 95, 109, 127, . . .
9. 61, 59, 55, 49, 41, . . .
10. 13, 3, −11, −29, −51 . . .

PART 3: Find the *nth* term of the sequence in the form $an^2 + bn + c$. Shade in the 10th term.

11. 6, 16, 30, 48, 70, . . .
12. 9, 13, 19, 27, 37, . . .
13. 5, 11, 19, 29, 41, . . .
14. 119, 115, 109, 101, 91, . . .
15. −95, −92, −87, −80, −71 . . .

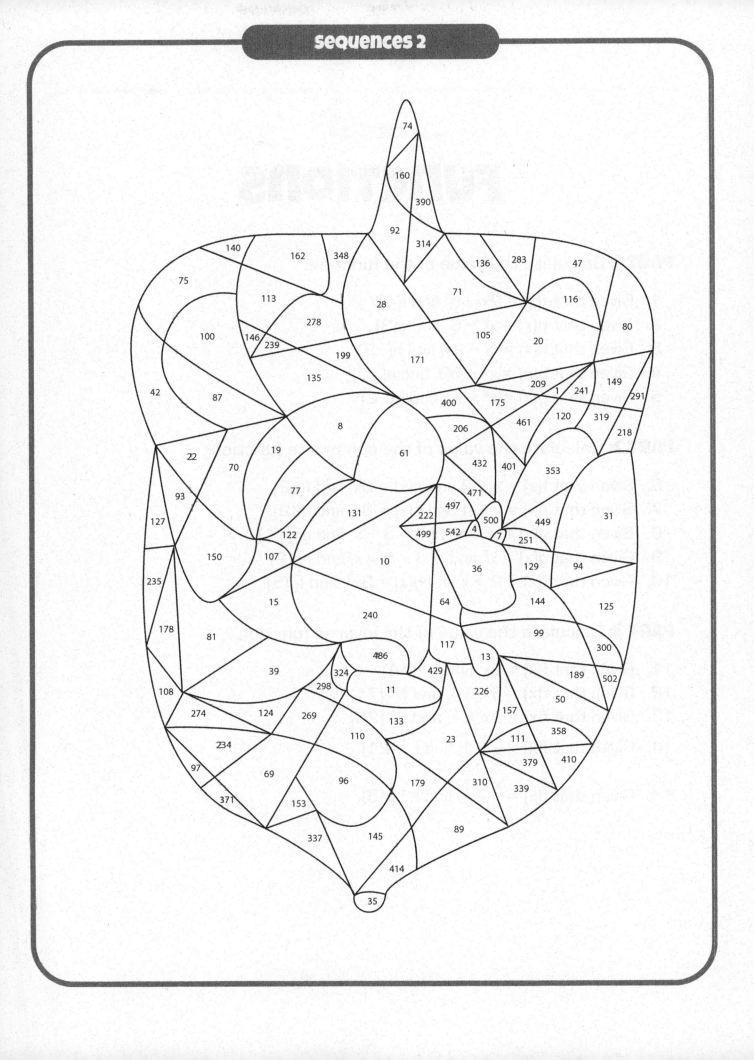

9

FUNCTIONS

PART 1: Calculate the value of the function.

1. Given that $f(x) = 2x - 6$, find $f(4)$
2. Given that $g(x) = x^2 - 6$, find $g(3)$
3. Given that $h(x) = 5 - 2x$, find $h(-2)$
4. Given that $h(x) = x^2 - 50$, find $h(10)$
5. Given that $g(x) = x^2 - x^3$, find $g(-2)$

PART 2: Calculate the value of the composite function.

6. Given that $f(x) = x + 2$ and $g(x) = 3x$, find $fg(2)$
7. Given that $f(x) = x - 4$ and $g(x) = 3x$, find $gf(9)$
8. Given that $g(x) = x^2$ and $h(x) = 3 - x$, find $gh(-1)$
9. Given that $g(x) = x^2$ and $h(x) = 5 - x$, find $hg(2)$
10. Given that $f(x) = 2 + x$ and $g(x) = 3x^2$, find $fg(5)$

PART 3: Calculate the value of the inverse function.

11. Given that $f(x) = 2x$, find $f^{-1}(14)$
12. Given that $f(x) = 3x - 4$, find $f^{-1}(71)$
13. Given that $f(x) = 2x + 1$, find $f^{-1}(23)$
14. Given that $f(x) = \dfrac{x}{2} + 1$, find $f^{-1}(21)$
15. Given that $f(x) = \dfrac{x + 1}{2}$, find $f^{-1}(45)$

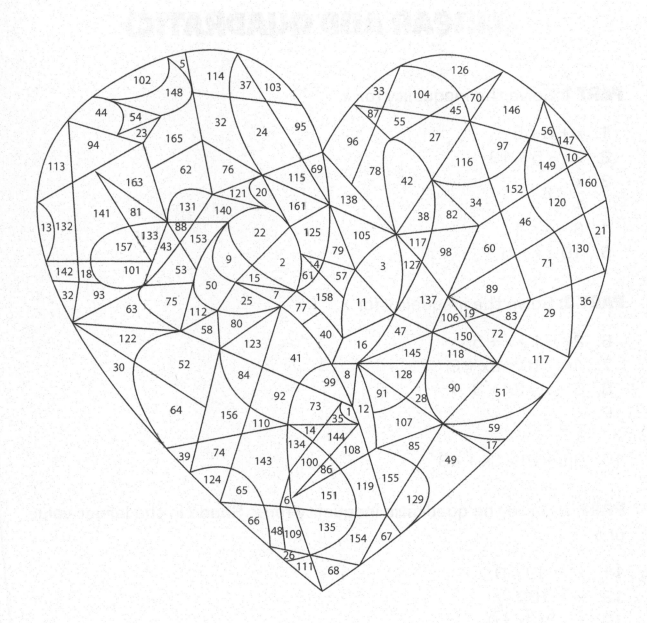

10

inequalities
(Linear and Quadratic)

PART 1: Solve the inequality for x.

1. $x + 3 < 5$
2. $3x - 5 < 19$
3. $\dfrac{x}{4} < 6$
4. $6 - x \leq 1$
5. $10 \geq x - 5$

PART 2: Solve the inequality for x.

6. $2x + 1 > x + 5$
7. $4x - 10 < 2x + 8$
8. $6 - x < 2x + 3$
9. $\dfrac{x}{3} \geq 8 - x$
10. $6(x + 2) > 3x + 48$

PART 3: Solve the quadratic inequality for x. Shade in the larger value of x.

11. $x^2 - 49 < 0$
12. $x^2 < 100$
13. $x^2 - 18x > 0$
14. $x^2 - x - 156 < 0$
15. $2x^2 - 67x + 155 > 0$

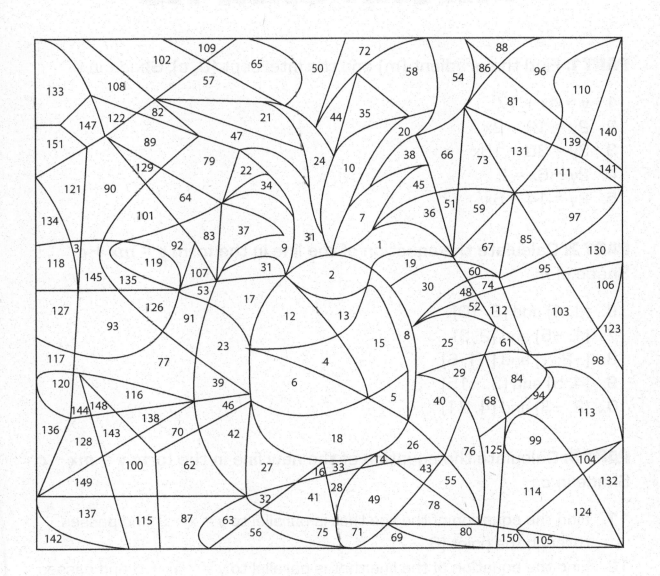

11

LINEAR GRAPHS

PART 1: Find the gradient (m) and the intercept (0, c). Shade in c.

1. $y = 4x + 17$
2. $2y = 12 - 2x$
3. $3y = 30 - 15x$
4. $2y - 6x = 2$
5. $2y = 14 - 6x$

PART 2: Calculate the equation of the line in the form $y = mx + c$. Shade in *m*.

6. (1, 4) and (3, 10)
7. (1, −5) and (2, 3)
8. (−2, 1) and (−1, 6)
9. (4, 5) and (3, −15)
10. (2, −3) and (4, 21)

PART 3: Calculate the equation of the new line in the form $y = mx - c$. Shade in *c*.

11. Find the equation of the line that is parallel to $y = x + 9$ and passes through the point (8, −7)
12. Find the equation of the line that is parallel to $y = -5x + 6$ and passes through the point (−3, 4)
13. Find the equation of the line that is perpendicular to $y = \frac{1}{5}x - 9$ and passes through the point (−5, −8)
14. Find the equation of the line that is perpendicular to $y = \frac{1}{5}x - 10$ and passes through the point (−1, 3)
15. Find the equation of the line that is parallel to $y - 2x = 1$ and passes through the point (4, −1)

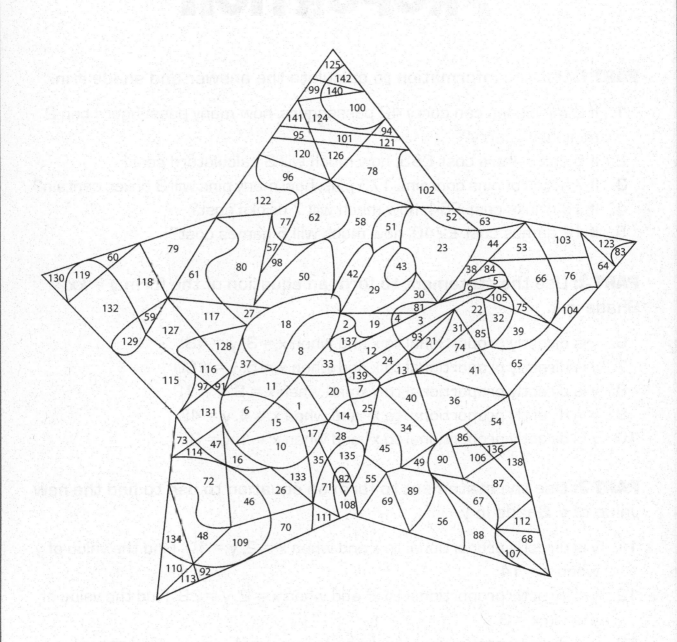

PROPORTION

PART 1: Use the information to calculate the answer and shade it in.

1. If 3 minibuses can carry 42 passengers, how many passengers can 2 minibuses carry?
2. If 5 calculators cost £65, how much will 3 calculators cost?
3. If 7 boxes of pins contains 175 pins, how many pins will 3 boxes contain?
4. If 18 drinks cost £54, how much will 7 drinks cost?
5. If 12 games cost £240, how much will 5 games cost?

PART 2: Use the statement to form an equation of the form y = *kx*. Shade in *k*.

6. y is directly proportional to x and when x = 3, y = 48
7. y is directly proportional to x and when x = 5, y = 100
8. y is directly proportional to √x and when x = 9, y = 12
9. y is directly proportional to x^2 and when x = 4, y = 48
10. y is directly proportional to x^3 and when x = 1, y = 8

PART 3: Use the statement to form an equation to use to find the new value of *y*. Shade in *y*.

11. y is directly proportional to x and when x = 2, y = 10. Find the value of y when x = 14
12. y is directly proportional to x^2 and when x = 2, y = 28. Find the value of y when x = 3
13. y is directly proportional to √x and when x = 4, y = 24. Find the value of y when x = 16
14. y is inversely proportional to x and when x = 14, y = 10. Find the value of y when x = 4
15. y is inversely proportional to x^2 and when x = 2, y = 75. Find the value of y when x = 5

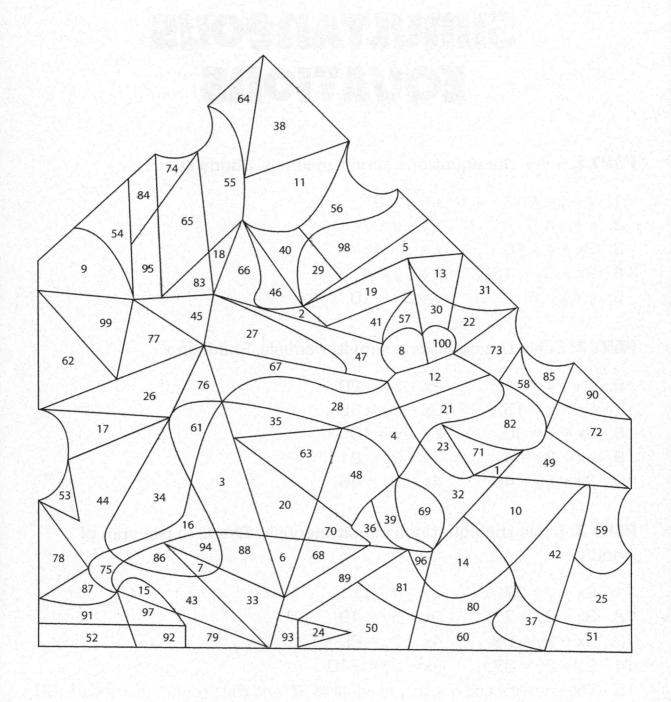

13

SIMULTANEOUS EQUATIONS

PART 1: Solve the equations simultaneously. Shade in x.

1. $x + y = 8$, $x - y = 2$
2. $x + y = 5$, $2x - y = 7$
3. $3x + y = 16$, $x + y = 4$
4. $2x + 3y = 12$, $2x - y = 4$
5. $y = x - 6$, $y = 3x - 10$

PART 2: Solve the equations simultaneously. Shade in x.

6. $x + 2y = 11$, $2x + 3y = 20$
7. $2x + y = 15$, $3x - 2y = 33$
8. $3x + y = 30$, $x - 2y = 10$
9. $2x + 3y = 4$, $3x + 2y = 21$
10. $3x + 5y = 49$, $4x - 3y = 46$

PART 3: Solve the equations simultaneously. Shade in the sum of x and y.

11. $2x + y = 37$, $x - y = -1$
12. $3x - 2y = 7$, $2x + 5y = 49$
13. $5x - 2y = 59$, $4x - 3y = 29$
14. $3x + 2y = 37$, $2x - 3y = -10$
15. The sum of x and double y is equal to 30 and the product of x and y is 88.

    There are two possible answers. Shade in the largest total of x and y.

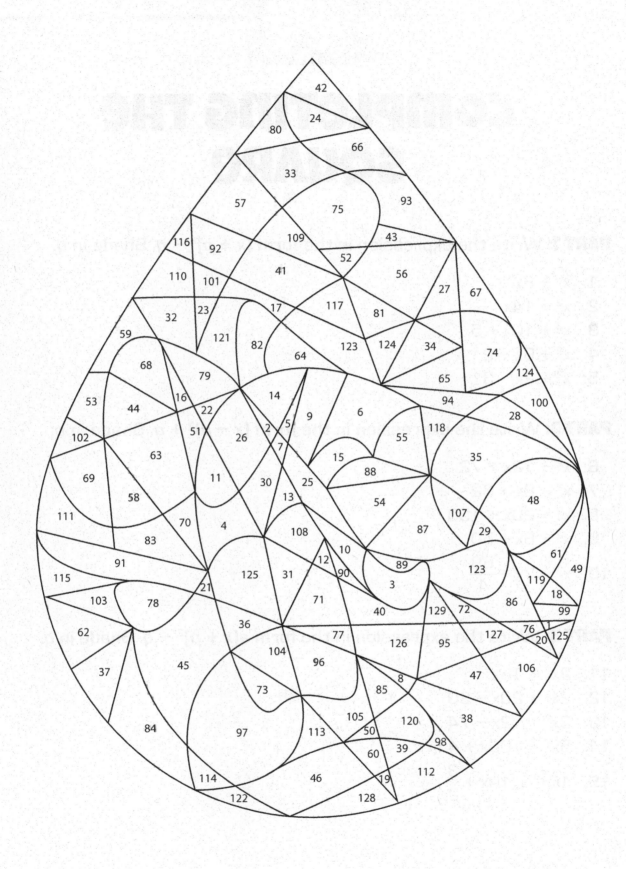

COMPLETING THE SQUARE

PART 1: Write the expression in the form $(x + p)^2 - q$. Shade in q.

1. $x^2 + 6x$
2. $x^2 + 14x$
3. $x^2 + 10x + 5$
4. $x^2 + 6x - 2$
5. $x^2 + 2x - 3$

PART 2: Write the expression in the form $(x - p)^2 + q$. Shade in q.

6. $x^2 - 12x + 72$
7. $x^2 - 8x + 32$
8. $x^2 - 20x + 150$
9. $x^2 - 6x + 50$
10. $x^2 - 7x + \dfrac{69}{4}$

PART 3: Write the expression in the form $a(x + p)^2 - q$. Shade in q.

11. $2x^2 + 16x$
12. $2x^2 + 20x - 30$
13. $3x^2 + 12x - 74$
14. $5x^2 + 100x + 417$
15. $10x^2 + 10x + \dfrac{3}{2}$

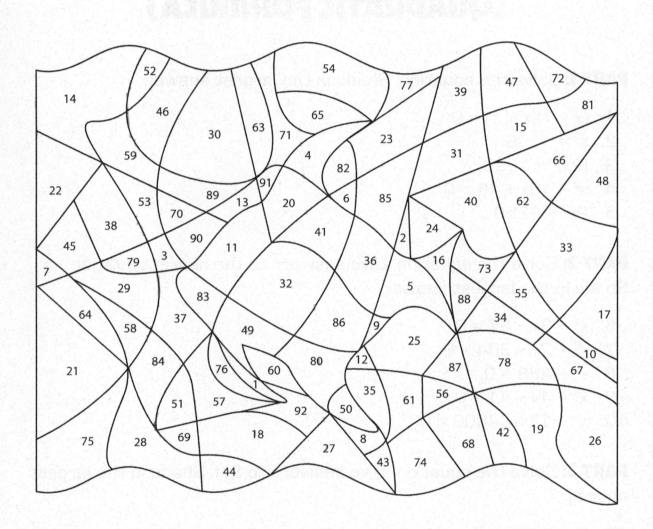

SOLVE THE EQUATION 4
(QUADRATIC FORMULA)

PART 1: Solve the equation. Shade in the largest answer.

1. $(x + 1)(x - 1) = 0$
2. $x^2 = 1156$
3. $(2x)^2 = 1296$
4. $x^2 - 10x + 16 = 0$
5. $2x^2 = 1250$

PART 2: Solve the equation. Give answers to the nearest integer. Shade in the largest answer.

6. $x^2 + 3x - 57 = 0$
7. $x^2 + 2x - 304 = 0$
8. $x^2 - 488 = 0$
9. $x^2 - 4x - 41 = 0$
10. $x^2 + 15x - 4600 = 0$

PART 3: Solve the equation. Give answers to 2sf. Shade in the largest answer.

11. $2x^2 - 196 = 9$
12. $2x^2 - 5x - 293 = 0$
13. $3x^2 + 2x - 4607 = 0$
14. $9x^2 + 12x - 17023 = 0$
15. $12x^2 + 5x - 33019 = 0$

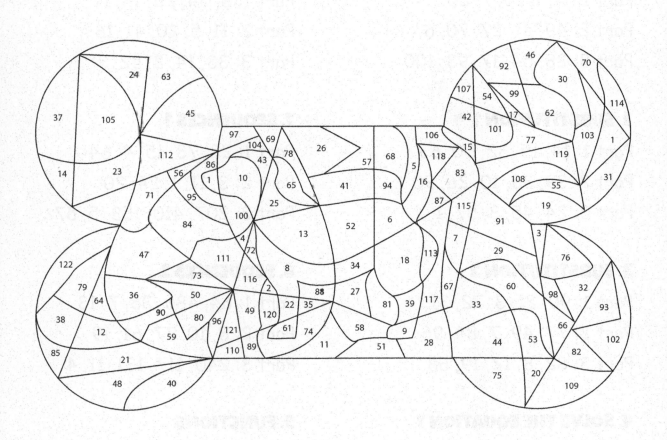

Answers

1. SIMPLIFYING
Part 1: 11, 1, 10, 7, 25
Part 2: 49, 41, 27, 70, 6
Part 3: 28, 54, 17, 93, 100

2. SUBSTITUTION 1
Part 1: 14, 15, 32, 50, 63
Part 2: 39, 36, 10, 26, 90
Part 3: 24, 45, 3, 57, 1

3. SUBSTITUTION 2
Part 1: 90, 21, 3, 72, 31
Part 2: 77, 49, 7, 84, 96
Part 3: 82, 8, 12, 19, 63

4. SOLVE THE EQUATION 1
Part 1: 7, 32, 71, 57, 12
Part 2: 38, 20, 24, 91, 70
Part 3: 4, 15, 44, 65, 40

5. SOLVE THE EQUATION 2
Part 1: 4, 13, 37, 74, 15
Part 2: 10, 18, 48, 90, 1
Part 3: 23, 57, 8, 66, 7

6. SOLVE THE EQUATION 3
Part 1: 8, 34, 25, 18, 1
Part 2: 11, 5, 20, 41, 16
Part 3: 33, 14, 2, 52, 3

7. SEQUENCES 1
Part 1: 22, 73, 15, 4, 64
Part 2: 3, 11, 1, 24, 20
Part 3: 207, 410, 153, 5, 57

8. SEQUENCES 2
Part 1: 64, 486, 36, 7, 13
Part 2: 8, 10, 77, 61, 19
Part 3: 240, 117, 131, 11, 4

9. FUNCTIONS
Part 1: 2, 3, 9, 50, 12
Part 2: 8, 15, 16, 1, 77
Part 3: 7, 25, 11, 40, 22

10. INEQUALITIES
Part 1: 2, 8, 24, 5, 15
Part 2: 4, 9, 1, 6, 12
Part 3: 7, 10, 18, 13, 31

11. LINEAR GRAPHS

Part 1: 17, 6, 10, 1, 7

Part 2: 3, 8, 5, 20, 12

Part 3: 15, 11, 33, 2, 9

12. PROPORTION

Part 1: 28, 39, 75, 21, 100

Part 2: 16, 20, 4, 3, 8

Part 3: 70, 63, 48, 35, 12

13. SIMULTANEOUS EQUATIONS

Part 1: 5, 4, 6, 3, 2

Part 2: 7, 9, 10, 11, 13

Part 3: 25, 14, 30, 15, 26

14. COMPLETING THE SQUARE

Part 1: 9, 49, 20, 11, 4

Part 2: 36, 16, 50, 41, 5

Part 3: 32, 80, 86, 83, 1

15. SOLVE THE EQUATION 4

Part 1: 1, 34, 18, 8, 25

Part 2: 6, 16, 22, 9, 61

Part 3: 10, 13, 39, 43, 52

SOLVED PUZZLES

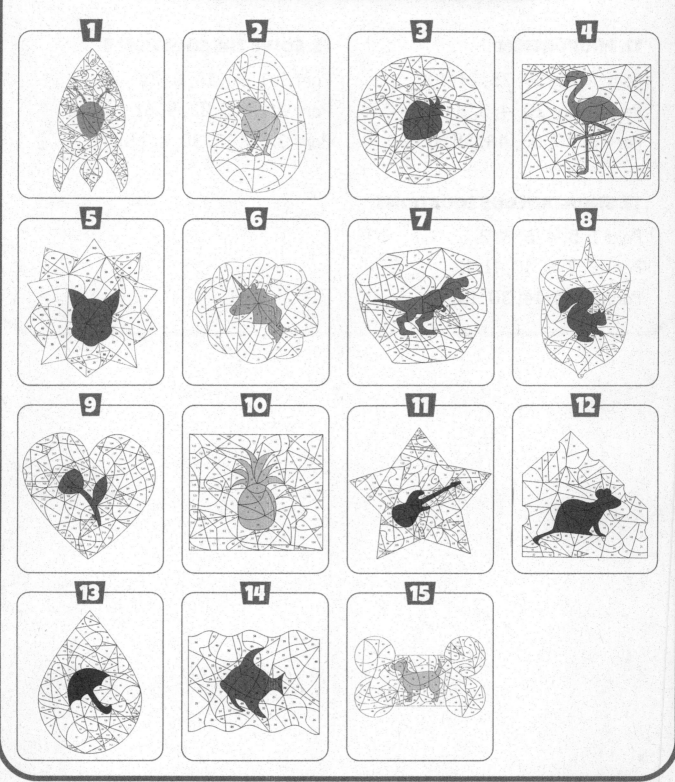